A Breath of S

Prepared for Developing our Communities,

Your Heritage Your Future

by

Members of the Hull and District Local History Research Group

2007

First published 2007

© Developing our Communities,
Your Heritage Your Future

Text by members of the Hull & District Local History Research
Group

All photographs © respective owners as indicated

Published by
Developing our Communities,
Your Heritage Your Future
In association with The Hull & District Local History Research
Group

ISBN
978-0-9556707-0-1

Printed and bound by
Artyfax Limited

'A Breath of Sculcoates'

An Introduction

Life is so fast moving and complicated these days that even the lives that our parents lived as children is now a dim and distant memory. This book opens a window in to that past, allowing us just a glimpse of how we used to live and a flavour of the people who inhabited that world.

In Sculcoates we have always been a cosmopolitan community, with a proud heritage of shipping and industry, right from the earliest days with Skuli the Dane the vibrant mix of people have knitted together to give us some amazing and influential characters.

Take a moment, turn the page and bring to life again the past with its buildings, people and community that once was Sculcoates.

Fran McStay

Chair

Sculcoates Neighbourhood Association

June 2007

CONTENTS

CITY CHILD

There are not many trees down the once green lane
And no swimmers now in 'Barmy Drain'.
For Sculcoates Lane is changing, from Melwood down to Air Street.
And children who once lived there, they all knew as their street.

Now, town planners call it 'progress' but they pull the buildings
down,
Houses, shops and terraces-all part of my home town.
In those 'villas' and 'groves', as children we played,
We cherished a childhood and memories were made.

Our pleasures were quite simple, yet never at a loss,
Climbing lamp-posts, playing hop-scotch, or a game of pitch and
toss.
Only poverty was plentiful (we could not ask for much),
If one had had a football, we would play at 'flag-edge touch'.

We had to make our own amusement, it's a fact our toys were few-
Whip and top, and marbles, stick and booler too.
In December, 'Winter warmers', just a tin of glowing rags,
And in summer, coloured crayons, to chalk upon the flags.

A game of relievo-(one, two, three), 'block' or bat and ball,

And oft went 'window tapping' just as night began to fall.

Many a happy hour we spent, although we got few treats,

Playing 'I draw snake' and 'rounders' in those shady gas-lit streets.

Now, they call it re-development,

But, in a high rise flat,

Can any child of modern times

Have memories like that?

by Albert Rollinson

THE ORIGINS AND DEVELOPMENT OF SCULCOATES

Viking Warrior
An early Sculcoates resident?
Humberside County Council

The beginnings

One thousand years ago the area to the north of Hull which is now Sculcoates was a remote, sparsely populated, and low-lying area of salt marshes with very little fresh water. It was badly drained and regularly flooded from the waters of both the River Hull and the River Humber. Sometime in the mid-twelfth century it is thought that a settler, possibly Danish and called Skuli began a settlement known as 'Skuli's Cottages' on the west bank of the River Hull, one mile north of its conflux with the River Humber. Skuli was a Danish name and as the word 'cote' means an enclosure for sheep and cattle it is very likely that Skulecote eventually became Sculcotes. Other variations of the name include Scowcots and Scowlcots. Sculcoates is not mentioned in the Domesday Book but what is more certain is that between 1160 and 1162 Benet de Sculcoates is recorded as being involved with William de Stuteville in the course of making ditches on the common pasture of Sculcoates to drain the marsh of Cottingham. In 1210-1220 the monks of Meaux grazed sheep on the pasture of Sculcoates, indicating that drainage was making the fields more habitable.

A manor house was recorded in Sculcoates by 1346 and in the same year a Mr. John Grey received permission to fortify it. The house still stood on the river bank in the seventeenth century but had disappeared by the 1780s. About this time a dozen or so houses and a windmill had been built along a road which ran close to the River Hull between the Charterhouse and the original ancient parish church of St. Mary's at Sculcoates, which had first been mentioned in 1232. This church was demolished in 1760 and a new one built on the same site. The road at the Charterhouse end was called Wincolmlee and at its Sculcoates end Church Street, names which remained until the late nineteenth century when Wincolmlee ran as far as Bankside.

Records of the little settlement of Sculcoates show that in 1337 only nineteen adults were paying the poll tax. In 1574 just seven taxpayers are recorded and in 1672 fifteen households were paying the hearth tax, levied between 1662 and 1679 and charged at two shillings for each hearth in a house. The population slowly increased and in 1743 eighty-eight families were counted as living in Sculcoates. Nothing is known about the agricultural progress of the area after the twelfth century mention of the common pastures but a seventeenth century map shows meadows called Great Ings and Little Ings, ings meaning 'a pasture by a stream', lying on the west and east sides of Beverley Road. The map shows the three-field pattern of arable farming with the large West Field lying between the river Hull and Beverley Road. The land was enclosed by the late seventeenth century and by 1691 there were fourteen principal landowners. Wilmington and Stepney were both hamlets within the parish of Sculcoates.

Beverley Road

After the foundation of Kingston-upon-Hull in 1293 plans were made to build roads leading from the new town and one of these was to be a highway between Hull and Beverley, running in a north-westerly direction. This road was to be sixty feet wide and work began in 1305. This was by no means a road in the modern sense of the word and was little more than a green lane. The reason for its sixty feet width was to enable travellers and wheeled vehicles to get around the obstacles caused by rutting and poor maintenance.

The road would have been regularly damaged by flooding and as, at that time, roads eventually had to be maintained by the parishes they ran through, Sculcoates would have been affected by this. Some repairs were made to local roads with funding from private legacies and charities, and Beverley Road would have no doubt benefited from these sources. Despite this the roads were very primitive and often impassable, especially during the winter months. Things improved considerably when the Hull to Beverley Turnpike Trust opened in 1744, the first of many such roads in the East Riding area. Under an Act of Parliament a Turnpike Trust could be formed by a number of interested businessmen and landowners who would constitute a body of trustees who in turn would contribute the funds for the improvement of a stretch of road. Toll charges could be made for the use of the road and most of the money raised would pay for the maintenance of the road. In the case of the Beverley turnpike, toll bars were positioned at Stepney, Newland, near the present Haworth Arms, and at Woodmansey, along with distinctive toll houses housing the family who were authorised to collect the tolls and issue the tickets. Turnpike roads were generally constructed of compressed stone chippings and were a great improvement to the old roads but they were still far from perfect and prone to damage. The road building methods of John Louden MacAdam had a great effect on turnpike roads which were the beginning of really modern roads. One of the distinctive features of turnpike roads were the milestones, often of different designs, and many are still in evidence in East Yorkshire and elsewhere. If one is travelling along a road nowadays which have such milestones you can be certain that you are on an old turnpike road. The Hull to Beverley Turnpike trust operated until 1871 when the maintenance of the road became the responsibility of the local Highway District Authority, and after 1888 of the County Council.

Frederick Needler
Courtesy of R. Needler

NEEDLER'S

Needler's was founded by Frederick Needler who was born on 12th December 1864 at Arnold, near Skirlaugh. His parents were George and Jane who married at All Saints Church, Sculcoates in April 1860. There seems to be mis-spelling, at some point, of the family name as the name recorded on his parents marriage certificate and on Fred's birth certificate is Needley. This changes on documents to Needler after 1865. Fred had a brother, John Henry and two sisters, Selina and Lucy.

At the time of the 1871 census the family resided in Argyle Street in the St. John's Wood area of Hull situated between Pearson Park and Cottingham Road. This street was off Queens Road and was re-named Maple Street in the 1880s.

George Needler's occupation was given as a colour maker so he was probably employed at this time in one of the local paint factories. George died of typhoid at home on 27th September

1872 aged 37 years. George's widow Jane was left with a young family to support and, although living in one of the better areas of Hull, it was rumoured in the family that she took in washing (in the 1881 census her occupation is shown as a laundress). Fred Needler attended St. John's school Newland. He left as soon as he was able and his first job was in a tea and coffee warehouse on High Street around 1878, he is described as being a grocer's apprentice in the 1881 census.

A shop opened around 1910 at 28 King Edward Street. This became well known between the wars with regular demonstrations of hand-piping of chocolates and Easter Eggs. Unfortunately the shop was destroyed in the 1941 air-raids and never re-opened.

At the age of 18 Fred was offered a job as a book-keeper by Mr Edward Buckton who had a small confectionery manufacturing business in the Paragon Station area. Mr Buckton's business ran into financial difficulties and in 1886 the plant was offered to Fred for £100.

Fred's mother bought the equipment for him with her savings. Fred then took on premises in nearby Anne Street where he employed two staff, a sugar boiler and a boy called Watson. A horse and cart was used for making deliveries. Fred's business was one of many of this type in Hull at the time.

Fred Elwell, the well known Beverley artist painted a picture of the staff in the factory dining room which was shown in the Wembley Empire Exhibition in 1925. This was seen by Edward, Prince of Wales who requested to visit the factory on an official visit to Hull in 1926. Sadly this painting has since been destroyed.

Fred worked very hard, with help also from his sister Lucy. He moved into the wholesaling trade and had various premises in an area to the north of Paragon Station. In 1890 he took over a property at 48a, Brook Street and in 1893 added 37 Brook Street. Eventually larger premises were bought in Spring Street for £900.

Fred Needler was a conscientious man with little time for any other interests apart from work. He was, however, a regular attendee at the Methodist Church, being a Sunday School teacher at the United Methodist Chapel, near Stepney Railway Station on Beverley Road. Many chocolate and confectionery firms were started by families with Methodist or Quaker origins, e.g Cadbury's and Fry's, they believed in the promotion of confectionery in their fight against the evils of alcohol.

Fred married Gertrude Wood in 1898, also a Sunday

School teacher, at Stepney Chapel, her family having originated from Shepley near Huddersfield. Fred and Gertrude had one child called Arthur Percival, born on 18th August 1900, who eventually took over as managing director on Fred's death in 1932.

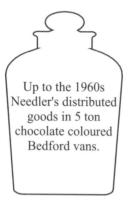

Up to the 1960s Needler's distributed goods in 5 ton chocolate coloured Bedford vans.

Frederick was a strong supporter of the Liberal Party and also generous to charities and family members. A house in Cottingham was donated to the Hull University for use as a student hall of residence (Needler Hall).

By the turn of the century the company was regarded as more than just a local sweet factory, producing 38 lines of boiled sweets, 40 of toffees, 35 lines of health sweets, 14 types of pralines and 15 different labelled sticks of rock. The firm were also wholesalers for Fry's, Cadbury's, Rowntree's, Craven's and Taverner's. A considerable boost to the sales was made by using clear glass jars instead of green ones which gave a better view of the contents. In 1902 the first Limited Company was formed as Fred Needler Ltd. Continued expansion meant that the Spring Street factory was too small, consequently larger premises were sought. In 1906 a larger factory was built on land which had belonged to a builder named Christie who had a yard off Sculcoates Lane. The new factory originally consisted of a two storey office block with an entrance off Lotus Avenue, (a terrace of houses off Bournemouth Street) with a single storey factory behind. The house which stood in the yard was used as Mr Percival Needler's office, this was still there until the 1970s. At the same time as the move to the new factory the company became known as Needler's Ltd. Owing to an increasing demand for the manufactured sweets the wholesale operation ceased around 1912. By this time the product range included 576 lines which included 74 in chocolate.

Fred Needler had considered a move into chocolate production for some time and a new chocolate plant was set up in 1916.

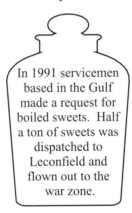

In 1991 servicemen based in the Gulf made a request for boiled sweets. Half a ton of sweets was dispatched to Leconfield and flown out to the war zone.

In the early 1920s the company employed 1700 mainly female staff, with more taken on a seasonal basis. In 1927 the factory packing areas were air conditioned so enabling sweet packing to continue in all weathers. Sweet wrappers were introduced in the 1920s when sweets were hand-wrapped, mechanical wrapping commenced in 1928.

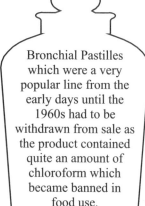

Bronchial Pastilles which were a very popular line from the early days until the 1960s had to be withdrawn from sale as the product contained quite an amount of chloroform which became banned in food use.

Glass jars would be collected and returned to the factory for sterilisation and re-use. Back in the 1930's when many families in the area were quite poor the children would hope to find sweets left in the jars, if they found any the drivers would let them have them.

In 1938 the Company's chemists found a way of producing clear fruit drops, known as Glace fruits, that became unrivalled until the mid 1960s. By this time the main production had moved away from chocolate towards sweets.

Until 1918 goods were delivered locally by horse and cart or van and nationally by rail. This system was unsuitable to meet the rising volume of orders, a fleet of delivery vans was therefore built up which by 1927 totalled 40 vans. In 1950 rail distribution ceased and transportation was made by road instead.

In 1958 Needler's became a publicly quoted Company with the Needler family retaining a controlling interest. Percival Needler was succeeded as Managing Director, upon his retirement in 1970 by his son Raymond. At this point the firm took over Batgers toffee manufacturers (famous for the Jersey toffee brand). Chocolate production which was heavily loss-making stopped in 1976. In 1980 the firm acquired a small confectionery manufacturer called Dickson, Orde and Co. based in Surrey. Also in the early 1980's export markets were opened up.

Needler's was always known for looking after its workforce with profit sharing and pension schemes from the early days. There were also good social and sports facilities. At one stage the company had a bungalow in Chestnut Avenue, Withernsea for use of the staff for holidays.

In 1986 Needler's was taken over by Hillsdown Holdings, a large meat company diversifying into other areas. Their anticipated development into a large confectionery group did not occur after the purchase of Bluebird Toffee was found to be a mistake. After Raymond Needler's retirement in 1987, Needlers was bought out by Nora SA, the largest food group in Norway, who continued manufacturing boiled sweets on the Sculcoates Lane site, under the Needler brand name and also supermarket own brands.

Needler's was sold to Ashby Confectioners of Corby in 1999 but they were unable to restore profitability and they closed the Hull factory C 2003. The whole industry had changed rapidly from 1990 due to the demise of the traditional sweet shop and the dominance of the supermarkets resulting in the disappearance of smaller manufacturers.

Housing in Bournemouth Street was demolished in the 1972 slum clearance programme, whilst Needler's factory itself was still in production until the beginning of this century. The Company's name lives on in the road named Needlers Way, which is in the approximate location of where Bournemouth Street stood. The site of the factory is now part of the Urban Sensation Housing Development, (note the word sensation taken from the line of sweets of that name).

Catalogue - Christmas 1934
hand coloured
Courtesy of Brynmor Jones Library

Needler's van 1920
Courtesy of R. Needler

Site of Needler's factory
H & D LHG

16

CHARTERHOUSE

The Charterhouse is the most elegant building in the Sculcoates area. It is positioned on the North side of Charterhouse Lane, off Wincolmlee, with the accompanying Master's residence on the southside of the lane. Looking at the house today you see an elegant Georgian building, which could possibly have been the home of a wealthy family in the eighteenth century. This however, is not the case and the building held an important and influential position in Sculcoates.

In 1368 Michael de la Pole founded the Carthusian priory housing one of the strictest orders living the lives of hermits. The inhabitants followed a life of prayer and meditation and being based outside the city walls were surrounded by pastures and meadows with views looking over the gentle flow of the river and beyond to the wolds. By 1384, in the reign of Richard II, Michael founded to the east of the Priory an almshouse or hospice for thirteen men and thirteen women under the care of a priest known as the 'Master'. The Dissolution of Monasteries by Henry VIII was the reason why the priory had disappeared by 1539 leaving only the hospital buildings on the south side of the lane. The hospital became known as the Charterhouse because of its association with the Carthusian Priory. Throughout the Civil War, Hull supported the Parliamentarians. Situated beyond the city walls, the Charterhouse was in an area which the defenders of the town wished to prevent the Royalists from controlling. By the second siege in 1643 Lord Fairfax had taken the sensible defensive action of ordering the Charterhouse to be destroyed and earthworks to be built.

The end of the civil war saw the rebuilding of the site but by the eighteenth century the buildings had deteriorated to such an extent that they had to be demolished and by 1780 they had been replaced by the handsome building we can see today. The structure consists of a central block with two projecting wings. The main entrance consists of a central portico supported by pillars. Above this portal is a pediment and on the top of the roof is a circular turret of eight Ionic pillars, with a dome.

A large chapel takes up the centre of the building. There are two plain glass windows on the east and west walls and box pews on three sides. On the north wall is a semicircular pulpit with elaborate carved swags and entered by a door in the wall and staircase behind. In the late eighteenth century the only roadway to the house from the town was by Trippet and Charterhouse alley (now Charterhouse Lane). At the west end of the alley was a large gateway leading into the fields and gardens before Sykes Street was developed. On the opposite side of the road to Charterhouse is the Master's House and although constructed around 1780 still has sections constructed in 1663 by William Catlyn, the person responsible for Wilberforce House and Crowle House. The West Dutch Gable was reconstructed in its original form in 1954 to rectify damage caused by bombing in World War II. Behind the house is a large walled garden which contains an ancient mulberry tree that still yields a good crop of fruit each year. (One notable Master of Charterhouse was the Rev Andrew Marvell, father of the 'garden poet' Andrew Marvell, MP for Hull, born in 1621)

The nineteenth century saw the accommodation for people seeking shelter being increased and the site losing its views of green fields as it became progressively enclosed by industry. The building still survives into the twenty first century as an almshouse with accommodation for residents of the city nowadays in self contained flats, continuing its purpose as envisaged centuries earlier by its founder.

The Master's House 2007
H & D LHRG

The Pulpit in Charterhouse 2007
H & D LHRG

Charterhouse 2007
H & D LHRG

20

ST. MARY'S ANGLICAN CHURCH, SCULCOATES

This church was the ancient parish church of Sculcoates which was first mentioned in 1232 and stood at what is now the corner of Air Street and Bankside. The medieval church was replaced in 1760 by a new building, described as being in the Rococo Gothic style but essentially Classical. Alterations were made to the church during 1827-30, and in 1861-63 by William Botterill of Hull. The church was demolished in 1869 and a new one was built on the same site which opened in 1873. During this period the church was replaced as the parish church by the newly-built Church of All Saints in Margaret Street but was re-assigned in 1873 when it re-opened. This church was demolished during 1915-16 when the present church was opened some distance further down Sculcoates Lane. The new building incorporated many artefacts from the old church including pillars, furniture, stained glass and monuments. Within the graveyard of the old church the church tower was still visible in 1956.

A visit to the old cemetery shows that many of the old gravestones have been removed but despite the overgrown condition of the cemetery many are still accessible and contain some interesting descriptions. Several contain the words 'his end was peace' while one very eloquent one states 'she opened her mouth with wisdom and her tongue was the law of kindness'.

An extension to the cemetery was consecrated in 1868 and although this is also overgrown it contains many fine monuments to the mariners and merchants of Hull. In sharp contrast to these are two sections of very small gravestones which are numbered and are more weathered than the others. One group of stones is dated around 1918 and the other around 1925. These graves are close together and often contained the remains of up to three people, not always from the same family. It appears that these small gravestones were of people who had died whilst in the Sculcoates Union Workhouse and were in fact pauper's graves. Child mortality was quite high in the eighteenth and nineteenth centuries and one grave contained both parents, a daughter aged twenty, and six children who died in their infancy. One tombstone dated 1797 was for a Lincolnshire farmer and was inscribed 'Life how short. Eternity how long'. There is a large patch of overgrown land which was the site of the original church. The path to the church door is still in evidence and is made up of old tomb slabs. A later cemetery on the opposite side of the road is generally well kept.

The present Church

The present Church of St. Mary is situated further down Sculcoates Lane and opened in 1916. Prior to this, attendances at the old church were dwindling and were often cancelled, or held at fortnightly or monthly intervals during the winter months. During these periods services were held at the chapel at Hull Charterhouse, with wooden benches being brought from St. Mary's to cater for the larger congregation. The new church was much nearer the Beverley Road end of Sculcoates Lane and it was hoped that this would lead to a rise in attendances.

St. Mary's Church was designed by Mr. Temple Moore to seat 400 people and is constructed of red Lincolnshire bricks and Ancaster stone. The aisled interior is of fine proportions with two side chapels dedicated to St. Francis and St. Patrick. The Tuscan columns of the old church were re-used in the building of the north chapel. The church was incomplete after 1916 but was completed in 1925 by Mr. Leslie Moore.

A visit to the church can be very rewarding. The font, the gift of the Rev. W.J. Pearson who was the vicar in 1889, is a Georgian wine-cooler of c1717 which was originally in Hotham House. It is of dark grey and green speckled marble. It has a striking brass cover of a later date and has the inscription 'One Lord, One Faith, One Baptism'. The lectern in the Chapel of St. Francis is a fine piece of carved oak in the Gothic style and is a memorial to Norman G.M. Mason, who was killed in France on September 13th 1918 aged 26. The altar font in the same chapel is Jacobean, dating it between 1602-1625.

The pulpit, in dark oak, is fairly modest in size, octagonal in shape, and stands on a panelled plinth. The 150 year old organ, which is still played, was purchased from the King's Hall Chapel in Fountain Road, having previously been in a Methodist chapel in Scott Street which closed in 1910. The Chapel of St. Francis is of particular interest as the woodwork is by Thompson of Kilburn, the celebrated 'mouse man' and several of his 'mice' can be seen. Among the monuments in the church are some very interesting wall tablets from the former church, one of which is to Jane Delamotte of 1761 with an inscription totally in Byrom shorthand, a very rare piece indeed. Two more are by the famous Hull sculptor Thomas Earle.

The life of the church today

During the years of the 1950s and 1960s there was a strong community spirit around the church. Youth groups consisting of Club, Scouts and Cubs and Sunday School were all well supported, the Scouts and Cubs having a membership of between 50-60 people. The Sunday School had its annual outing and other activities, and there was also a church choir. Many people in the community were married at St. Mary's and there were many functions and gatherings in the Parish Hall on the corner of Folkstone Street. Sculcoates was a vibrant, lively industrialised part of the city and St. Mary's Church played an important part in the community. With the eventual closing of many industrial concerns in the last thirty years, coupled with the demolition of much of the housing in the area, Sculcoates was bound to change, although the recent re-development of the Needlers and Power Station sites may give Sculcoates Lane some much needed re-generation.

The present church is very well kept and is the living of the parish priest the Rev. John Leeman who is also very popular in other parts of the city. There is a small, mainly elderly but very dedicated congregation, and the emphasis is on 'High Church', the services being very traditional. The church still continues to function despite the fact that not many parishioners now live in the area and there is a need to encourage a renewal of community atmosphere and spirit. Services are held every Sunday at 11-00 am which is a sung Eucharist and the church is open for visitation on Mondays when a coffee morning is held. There is also a Mass at 4-00 pm each Monday.

Other churches in Sculcoates parish

There are other places of worship within the parish of Sculcoates. A Church of England one is St. Paul's Church in St. Paul's Street/Bridlington Street. The original church was built in 1847 by William Hey Dykes and was demolished in 1976. The present church was built on the same site by R.G. Sims.

St. Charles Borromeo Roman Catholic Church in Jarrett Street is a beautiful church which was constructed in 1828-29 by John Earle Junior and greatly altered in 1854 by Smith, Broderick and Lowther. The central Corinthian porch was added in 1894.

The Elim Pentecostal City Temple (Congregational) on Princes Avenue was built in 1898-99 to a design by W.H. Bingley and is a Gothic style building of red brick with stone dressings.

The Pentecostal Glad Tidings Hall (New Connexion Methodist) is on Beverley Road near the junction with Cave Street and was built in 1849. It is a Classical style building with a pedimented gable.

The Society of Friends Meeting House is on Percy Street in what was the former Albion House an mid-nineteenth century house which was converted for use by the Quakers about 1920.

Lost churches and chapels

Over the years there has been at least thirty-three old churches and chapels in Sculcoats of which most have sadly been lost forever. One that is still remaining is St. Gregory's Roman Catholic school/chapel of 1893 in Scott Street, a very large building situated on the corner of Lockwood Street and stretching down that street for some distance. The building was built by R.G. Smith and F.S. Broderick. The chapel is on the first floor with Gothic windows. The building is now used as a second hand pine furniture warehouse.

St Mary's Church interior 2007
H & D LHRG

26

CATTLE'S FINANCE – SHOPACHECK

Did you know John Cattle the financier started his empire in the
Sculcoates area?

He began in a little shop at the corner of Waterloo Street and
Brunswick Avenue selling children's clothes and drapery. It was a
poor working class area and he could arrange for the goods to be paid
for weekly.

He developed the shopping voucher system (the first credit card?) for
other shops as well as his own and the money to be collected weekly
by his agents. It was to become a common sight to see these men
running up and down the terraces and streets, particularly on a
Thursday and Friday, after the husband had received his wages. It
became quite a challenge and a victory if you could miss him!

Mr Cattle diversified into furniture, to be paid for weekly. He opened
shops on all the main roads, including Ewbanks furniture warehouse
and taking over Edwin Davis Department Store.

As 'one man' money lending businesses became available he would
purchase them thus increasing his turnover. He later made take-over
offers for larger companies to create the biggest consumer finance
firm in the country with branches in most cities. It is now listed on
the stock market as on of the top one hundred companies.

He never forgot his roots and became a Methodist benefactor for
King's Hall, Fountain Road, donating 150 Christmas hampers and
continental quilts to their pensioners every year.

You can still see mini buses for the disabled with 'Donated from the
Joe and Annie Cattle Trust' painted on the side.

He always had an interest in sport and became the sponsor of the Hull F.C. Rugby Club which for years had 'Shopacheck' emblazoned on their shirts.

SCULCOATES AND THE WHALING TRADE

It may not be generally known, but for a period during the 19th century the whaling trade played a significant part in the local economy. An advertisement from the Hull Advertiser and Evening Gazette of June 1812 confirms this by giving notice of an auction of a whale-yard situated on Sculcoates Lane. Known as Greenland yards, after the part of the world the local whalers fished in, this particular whale-yard was being sold by one Quanton Levitt who had recently become a bankrupt. According to the advertisement the yard covered just 3 acres and was made up of a riverside wharf, a boiling yard, a number of buildings and some cranes. The wharf was described as being constructed of red brick and 2,534 square yards in area, with an attached quay of 189 feet in length. At the Northern end of the wharf was situated a newly erected crane; with space for a second, and a warehouse, 127 feet in length and 26 feet in width. Also, and across on the Western side of Sculcoates Lane opposite the wharf, was situated a boiling house, 64 feet in length and 37 feet in width.

This building contained a copper vat, capable of boiling 4 ½ tons of whale oil, 3 lead coolers, and a crane fitted with a cast-iron wheel and barrel. Next to this building was situated a cooper's shop, 57 feet in length and 22 feet in width, and the foreman's dwelling house.

Situated on both sides of the River Hull in Sculcoates and Wilmington, and having a bad reputation for causing pollution, the role of the Greenland yards was to process the catches brought into Hull by the local whaling fleet. Cut up into small pieces and stored in wooden barrels, once a whaler arrived in port the now putrefying blubber, along with whalebone, baleen, and other useful parts of the whale would be transferred into lighters in the river mouth or the Old Harbour. It would then be carried up to the Greenland yards where it would be unloaded by crane and transported into a boiling house. Here the blubber would undergo a prolonged boiling process in order to produce whale oil, or train oil as it was also known. Used, amongst other things for lighting, as a lubricant, and in the production of paints and soap, whale oil was a highly versatile and sought after product. Each whale could produce up to 20 tons of oil, which in turn could sell for between £20 and £50 per ton. The remainder of the lighter's cargo such as whalebone and baleen would be processed in an open space within the yard. Regarded as "the plastic of the 18th and 19th centuries" whalebone had countless uses with many local industries reliant upon it as a raw material.

Although the origins of local whaling can be traced back to 1598, when a group of merchants specially fitted out a ship for an expedition to the seas around Iceland, the industry didn't start to flourish until the 18th century. Then in 1733 the British government, wishing both to end the reliance on imported whale products and encourage the growth of the British whaling industry, introduced a bounty, or subsidy of 20 shillings per ton burthen on all ships fitted out for whaling. The sum subsequently increased to 30 shillings per ton in 1740 and 40 shillings per ton in 1750. In 1776 the government also introduced a duty on all imported oil and whalebone, which encouraged the home industry even further.

The catalyst behind the growth of the whaling industry in the port of Hull at this time was one Captain Samuel Standidge (1725-1803). Born in Bridlington, he had been the master of a number of Hull vessels in both the North American and Baltic trades since the 1750s. Then, in 1766, he purchased and fitted out a vessel of 315 tons called the 'Berry' for a whaling expedition to the seas of Greenland. Considered at the time to be a most foolhardy and hazardous venture, the 'Berry' however sailed on 9th April 1766 under Captain J. Hall, and a crew of 2 mates, 1 surgeon, 1 carpenter, 1 bosun , 5 harpooners, 5 boat steerers, 6 line managers, 20 seamen, 1 cooper and apprentice. She returned to Hull on 10th August of the same year with a catch of 1 whale and 400 seals, their skins being sold for 5 or 6 shillings each. This was a most remarkable feat, as before then the skins of seals had generally been thrown overboard, they having an intrinsic value of no more than 3d. each. As a result of this successful voyage Captain Standidge sent 2 more whalers to the same waters a year later, with a further 3 vessels following them in 1768. Many others followed his example in the years ahead, with Standidge offering his help and assistance at every turn. Regarded by many as a man of exceptional qualities he was made Sheriff of Hull in 1775, became Mayor in 1795, and was knighted for services to British shipping.

By 1785 6,600 men and women were employed in Hull's whaling industry, but the industry was yet to reach its peak. This occurred in 1820, when 60 vessels returned from Greenland and the Davis Strait with the produce of 688 whales. Earning the huge sum of £318,880, this worked out at more than £5,000 per ship. However, in 1821 a disaster befell the Hull fleet that was to signal the decline of the local industry. Of the 61 vessels which left the port that year 9 where lost, smashed into pieces by the Arctic ice. This event, combined with a fall in the price of whale oil, a reduction in the government bounty, and the availability of more attractive investments, caused many investors to withdraw their capital. By 1830 the number of whalers in the Hull fleet had fallen to only 33, and due to a serious decline of stocks off Greenland, everyone of these was now fishing in the Davis Strait. Unfortunately, disaster was again to beset the fleet. Described as "the most disastrous year in the annals of British whaling", of the 91 British ships whaling in this area 19 were wrecked and almost all of the others were damaged. Out of the Hull ships, 6 were wrecked, and 8 returned home without a single catch. This caused so much financial distress, the City's Mayor held a meeting at the Guildhall in order to open a fund for the whalers' crew and their families. By 1835 the Hull fleet had declined yet again to only 23 vessels, a year later this figure had fallen to 15, and in 1837 the figure fell to a mere 11 ships. This trend continued until 1842 when the Hull whaling fleet was to consist of only 2 vessels, namely the 359 ton 'Jane' and 294 ton 'Truelove'.

The latter vessel was perhaps the most famous Hull whaler of all time. Built in 1764 as a merchant vessel in Philadelphia the 'Truelove' was used during the War of Independence as a privateer, until captured by a British warship. Then in 1780 she was purchased from the British Government by one John Voase, a Hull wine merchant and shipowner, who employed her in the wine trade between Oporto and Hull. She was to continue in this role until 1784, when after strengthening, she was to make her first whaling voyage to the seas off Greenland. In this trade she proved herself to be extremely successful in fact she was to make an incredible 72 voyages to the Arctic before her eventual retirement from whaling in 1868. During this period it has been estimated that she caught more than 500 whales, which in turn produced more than 5,000 tons of whale oil.

By 1846, with whale oil selling for £25 per ton and whalebone selling for £200 per ton, the Hull whaling fleet had partially recovered and now consisted of 15 ships. This state of affairs continued until 1853 when the industry started to decline. To counter this a number of steam-ships were introduced into the fleet, the first of these being the 355 ton 'Diana'. Originally built in Bremen in 1840, and first registered in Hull in 1856, her first voyage to the Arctic whaling grounds was as a sailing vessel.

However, in 1857 the bold decision was made to install a 40hp steam engine, making her the world's first steam powered whaler. Now able to move independently of the wind, she returned from her first voyage as a steam-ship in May 1857 with 140 tons of blubber, 1,300 seal skins, and 5 live seals.

Despite such innovation, by 1869 the 'Diana', under the command of Capt. Richard Wells, was the only vessel left whaling out of the port of Hull. Unfortunately, whilst returning from the Shetland Islands, she encountered appalling weather conditions off Spurn Point which resulted in her being driven ashore on the Sand Haile Flats on the Lincolnshire coast. Although all of her crew were eventually saved by local lifeboats, the 'Diana' herself became a total loss, and Hull's long association with whaling came to an end.

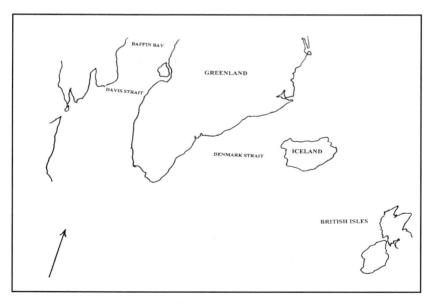

Northern whaling area
H & D LHRG

A link with the past
H & D LHRG

PARISH BOUNDARIES AND EXTENSION OF SCULCOATES

An early map of Sculcoates dated 1691 and redrawn in 1849 clearly shows the boundaries of the parish, which covered an area of 738 acres. Using modern landmarks the eastern boundary is the River Hull, with its southern end being the town walls, just south of the present North Bridge, and its northern end at Stoneferry. The northern boundary then ran from Stoneferry in a south-westerly direction, along streams, ditches and field boundaries, before crossing Beverley Road and carrying onwards along Queens Road to its junction with Prince's Avenue. It then became the western boundary along Prince's Avenue to its junction with Spring Bank before continuing along Spring Bank and into Prospect Street before meeting the town walls again at the Victoria Square end of Queens Gardens. The short southern boundary was the town walls running across the centre of what is now Queens Gardens. A quick look at a modern map will show what a very large area this is.

The expansion of Sculcoates

In 1774 the walls, ramparts and ditches which constituted the fortifications to the north and west of the town of Hull were granted to the Hull Dock Company for the construction of docks and harbour works and most of the town's defences were demolished. The Dock, later to be renamed Queens Dock, was opened in 1778 and at the time was the largest dock in the kingdom with a water area of ten acres plus 18,000 square yards of dock estate. The area to the north of the new dock was now ripe for development and expansion as people were eager to leave the cramped confines of the old town.

In 1778 the only building of any significance between Hull and Sculcoates was the ancient Charterhouse which had its origins in the Carthusian priory founded in 1368 by Michael de la Pole, which was situated less than a quarter of a mile north of the walled town of Hull. The priory was dissolved by King Henry VIII as part of the Dissolution of the Monasteries in 1536, re-established the following year and closed again in 1539 to become the Charterhouse Hospital, hospital being the name for an almshouse at that period. Much of the building was destroyed during the English Civil War when Hull was besieged but it was rebuilt on the same site during 1649-50. This building was in turn demolished in 1777 and rebuilt between 1778-80, and including several extensions between 1804 and 1888 comprises the buildings which still stand on Charterhouse Lane to the present day.

Over more or less the same period the church of St. Mary's at Sculcoates was also undergoing changes. The ancient church, which had stood at what is now the corner of Air Street and Bankside since 1232, was demolished in 1760 and a new one built on the same site. This church closed in 1870 and yet another opened on the site in 1872. The new church continued to serve the parish of Sculcoates until 1916, by which time the growth of Sculcoates had risen to a population of several thousand, many of them living too far from St. Mary's church. Other churches had been built in other parts of the parish and it was decided to build a new church, further along Sculcoates Lane and nearer to Beverley Road. This church opened in 1916 and was designed by Mr. Temple Moore and some of the fittings and fixtures of the old church were incorporated into the new one.

Development to the north of the new dock made rapid progress and the 'Northern Suburb' as it became to be known sprung up very quickly and between 1782 and 1792 many fine Georgian houses had been built as a residential area for merchants and professional people in Savile Street, Dock Street, George Street, North Street, Bridge Street and Charlotte Street. A study published by the University of Hull shows the status of the sixty-two inhabitants of these streets in 1791. Fifteen were merchants, twenty-six were master mariners or ship owners, four were professional gentlemen and seventeen were tradesmen or others. The beautiful Kingston Square, designed by Mr. John Jarrett was laid out in 1801 and off the western boundary of Prospect Street, Storey Street, Albion Street, Bond Street and Waltham Street were all laid out and populated by this time. All of this development, although known as the 'Northern Suburb', was in fact South Sculcoates, and by this time the Sculcoates Improvement Commissioners, created in 1801, were administering various public services within the parish.

Further expansion

From this time onwards it is possible to follow the growth of
Sculcoates by use of the many maps that were now becoming
available. The Baines map of 1823 shows that Beverley Road
was at that time called Beverley Street from its junction with
Spring Bank, with a few houses in the area now occupied by the
Hull Daily Mail, and with only scattered houses or farms along
the turnpike road. Grimston Street and Conduit Street ran north to
a junction with Cannon Street and Green Lane, with a few houses
in Boteler Street and Gibson Street further to the north. Boteler
Street would later become part of Grimston Street. On the banks
of the River Hull, Church Street showed the side streets of
Cumberland, Oxford and York Streets.

Goodwill and Lawson's 1853 plan of Hull shows the east side of
Beverley Road stretching up past Stepney Lane and on to
Sculcoates Lane which connected with Air Street and its junction
with Church Street. Conduit Street had become Worship Street
and ran as far as Caroline Street. Cotton Mill Street, soon to
become Barmston Street, is shown while Fountain Road has only
its east and west ends, with fields in between. The Sculcoates
Workhouse, later to become Kingston General Hospital is shown
at the corner of Fountain Road. Wellington Lane was the furthest
street to the north on the west side of Beverley Road and the name
Beverley Street had disappeared. In the central area of Sculcoates
Charles Street pushed as far north as Liddell Street and the
Kingston Cotton Mill of 1845 is shown. On the western boundary

Spring Bank now ran as far as its junction with Newland Tofts Lane, later to become Prince's Avenue and the Zoological Gardens of 1840 are laid out. Vane Street and Walmsley Street are shown at the town end of Spring Bank.

By 1880, Peck's plan of that year shows great expansion from east to west. There were many more side streets as far as Sculcoates Lane on the east side of Beverley Road and on the west side as far as Queens Road. Fountain Road was now complete and in the north-west corner of the parish the beautiful Pearson's Park of 1860 is now shown. To the west Spring Bank to Prince's Avenue now shows Morpeth Street, Hutt Street, formerly East Grove, and Peel Street, formerly West Grove. Albany Street and Louis Street are laid out and the Zoological Gardens are now built over. On Wincolmlee and Church Street practically all of the side streets of the present day are shown and the Sculcoates Bridge of 1875 crosses the River Hull linking Swann Street with Chapman Street in east Hull. In central Sculcoates the Charles Street alignment is continued from Liddell Street by the new Waterloo Street, which crosses Fountain Road and ends at its junction with Rose Street. The Victoria Dock railway line, which also carried the Hornsea and Withernsea lines, is shown as are the Botanic and Stepney stations of 1853.

Finally, the 1906 Bacon plan of Hull shows that the expansion of Sculcoates was almost complete and that the parish looked very much as it did forty years ago when re-development of the area began. Sculcoates Power Station is shown, as is the British Gas

Works, and the North Eastern Railway and the Hull and Barnsley railway lines cross the parish to the north. The Beverley Road passenger station on the Hull and Barnsley high level line is shown in Fitzroy Street as is the same company's passenger and goods station in Cannon Street. In the east the Scott Street Bridge of 1902/3 crosses the River Hull to link up with Jennings Street and St. Mark's Street into industrial east Hull. The ancient parish of Sculcoates was by now an integral part of Hull with many of its industries and much of its population within its boundaries.

INDUSTRIAL DEVELOPMENT OF SCULCOATES

In 1832 the boundaries of Hull were enlarged and a new Parliamentary Borough was created with the parish of Sculcoates placed within the new borough in 1837. Industrial development had also been taking place in Sculcoates, most of it close to the banks of the River Hull. Brewing of beer, sugar refining, ship building, weaving, wool-combing, and dyeing had all been recorded by the mid-eighteenth century. By 1818 there were more shipyards, a timber yard in Church Street, a glue manufactury and an iron-foundry in Cannon Street. According to the 'Hull Advertiser' of 1 August 1823 the first steam packet built at Hull was the 'Lowther' of 95 tons which was launched from M.&T. Robinson's shipyard, Sculcoates. In 1861 Thomas Holmes was employing forty-six men and boys in his tanning business while his brother William was employing twenty-five. The company later took the name of Thomas Holmes & Sons Ltd., a business which continued up to the final quarter of the twentieth century. In the 1850s Thomas Holmes was working with Joseph Henry Fenner on a project that led to the patenting of improved driving belts for machinery. The subsequent success of J.H. Fenner & Company Ltd. evolved from this partnership. An unusual business for East Yorkshire, that came to Sculcoates in 1845, was the Kingston Cotton Mill situated in Cumberland Street at its junction with Fountain Road. This was a huge building of five storeys high and a length of five hundred feet on an eleven acre site. The business carried on until 1894 when the company went into liquidation. In 1864 Frederick Needler started a confectionery business specialising in the production of boiled sweets and in the early twentieth century fifty workers were employed in a factory in Spring Street. In 1906 a new factory was built in Sculcoates Lane while the manufacturing of chocolate was also added to the business. The factory closed in the final quarter of the century and the premises were subsequently demolished. The site has recently been developed for housing and is now called Needlers Way. In 1898 Hull acquired one of its most distinctive landmarks when the Sculcoates Power Station was opened on the 24 October of that year. Built on the western bank of the Barmston Drain in Sculcoates Lane the power station played an important part in Hull's industrial and social progress as electricity became more important in the early decades of the twentieth century. The station closed down in 1976 and was demolished by 1981. It also is being developed for housing and is now called Abbey Way. Both of these new housing developments have brought much needed regeneration to the Sculcoates Lane area.

As industry grew in Sculcoates the demand for cheap housing for the workers employed in them became greater and they were mainly housed in the side streets to the east of Beverley Road and west of the River Hull. The contrast between these houses and those in the 'Northern Suburb' could not have been greater. Many of the houses were built before housing legislation came in with the Kingston upon Hull Improvement Bill of 1854, and would have been built with just one course of bricks. As in other working-class areas of Hull many of them would have been built in crowded off-street courtyards with tunnel entries. The living conditions were generally bad, the streets in the Bankside and Wincolmlee areas were prone to flooding and sanitation and drainage was very poor. Above all, the ever pervading smell of local industry from tan-yards and oil-mills etc, along with the obnoxious smells of the 'muck-garths', where the 'night-soil' was processed for manure. hung in the air. It could have been no surprise therefore that the Hull cholera epidemic of 1849 affected Sculcoates greatly and it was only after this outbreak that some signs of improvement slowly appeared in public health matters. Further westwards the streets had a better class of house as most of these were built after 1854 and many were also private houses. As Sculcoates moved into the twentieth century its development was virtually complete and little change was seen until the re-development programmes of the third quarter of the century, improvements we are all familiar with and which are on-going today.

REFLECTIONS ON SCULCOATES RESIDENTS' MEMORIES

'...my parents and five children lived in a sham four, that is a two up and a two down' (Sculcoates resident)

When Queen Victoria came to the throne in 1837 most of her English subjects were country folk, when she died in 1901 most of them were townspeople. Hull followed that trend, as in 1841 the population stood at 65,670, sixty years later it had increased by 173,847 to 239,517. With such an increase in a relatively short time scale more houses were needed to meet a soaring demand for accommodation in Hull. Whenever there is a chance to make a quick profit exploiters will try to take advantage of the situation, house builders were no exception.

Working class houses in the nineteenth century were built by small builders with inadequate resources, the inevitable result being poor quality homes constructed with inferior materials, a type of building becoming known as jerry-built. The phrase jerry-built seems to have originated in Liverpool about 1830 as a corruption of jury mast or jury-rigging, the temporary or makeshift replacement in an emergency. Another possibility being the name connected with Jericho, the walls of which came tumbling down at the sound of trumpets.

The consequence of building these inferior houses resulted in legislation being enacted in the latter half of the nineteenth century. All dwellings had now to be constructed, at least to the minimum standards laid down by these regulations, becoming known as bylaw houses. An architect drawing dated 1894 shows 19-27 Tunis Street, comprising of two rooms down stairs and two up with the door of one room opening directly onto the street, these basic four room dwellings were known as sham fours. Bylaw houses built to these standards were an improvement on previous working class houses; nevertheless, these dwellings would be unacceptable today. The walls were one brick thick so no cavity for insulation, double-glazing was unknown, window frames were not hinged; they slid up and down in grooves, a type known as sash windows, coal gas provided lighting and power for a gas cooker.

Solid fuel for the open fires was stored in a small brick outhouse next to the W.C. whose doors, made out of floor boards, had gaps at the top and bottom resulting in visits to the W.C. being kept to a minimum during inclement weather and night time. In a winter the water supply froze in the pipes for days on end, then when the thaw came pipes burst, the water shortage with its consequences are not pleasant to contemplate. Toilet paper was usually the Hull Daily Mail cut to an appropriate size, threaded on a piece of string nailed to the door.

In 1920 there were still about 27,575 privies not connected to main drainage, 13,741 had pail closet and in a further 10,966 dwellings had to have their contents carried through the house as they had no rear entrance. The euphemism for this human waste being night soil as it was collected at night by the 'wet' dustmen in horse drawn carts, then deposited in muck-garths, imagine the smell and the flies. When sanitary reformers wanted every dwelling to have a water closet, which seemed like a good idea, the night soil collectors, who sold the pail's product to farmers as manure, objected to more W.C. s being fitted, claiming it would adversely affect their livelihood. The last privies in Hull were not removed until the 1950s.

The water supply to many older houses in Sculcoates came from a standpipe in the rear concrete yard making heating water on the fire or gas hob a time consuming chore. Bath night in most working class homes was traditionally carried out on a Friday night in a galvanised tub in front of the fire; the tub hung on a nail fastened to the wall when not in use. After bathing the watery contents needed to be bailed out as the bath became too heavy to lift. Hot, clean water was at a premium, the first one bathing being the most fortunate. However, this inconvenience with bath water paled into insignificance when the weekly wash came round on a Monday. Provision for heating the water took place in a large metal container (the copper) with a fire place beneath, situated in the corner of the scullery, the fire needed to be lit early in the morning in preparation for a long day ahead.

Before synthetic fibres came along natural materials tended to hold more water after soaking in a dolly tub. The upmarket ones had a high back for scrubbing after they had been twisted and turned by hand with dolly legs, a tiring process particularly with heavy wet natural materials, then put through a mangle.

Soapflakes were expensive so soda softened the water, then soap that came in long squares that needed cutting provided the lather.

Stubborn stains in materials needed to be scrubbed with soap and a stiff brush, then rinsed manually, a process that did not treat hands kindly before domestic rubber gloves arrived.

Apart from rain, hanging the clothes out to dry posed a problem as the pall of smoke that hung over the district deposited soot everywhere including freshly washed clothes, taking them indoors to dry round the fire made the room uncomfortable to use on wash day. Two flat irons heated on the fire or gas ring were used for ironing and as no thermostatic controls existed in those days, one test for the correct temperature was when the user's spit bounced off the irons face it was ready for use.

Speculative house builders were adept at utilising the minimum amount of land to gain its maximum financial potential. The houses may have been packed together too close for comfort, however, it did allow the dwellings to have a comparatively low rent. Sculcoates, like many other similar areas in Victorian and Edwardian times was virtually a self-contained community within a city.

Most of life's amenities such as churches, shops, schools and a place of work were close to home and consequently the majority of the population who were born in Sculcoates, lived, played worked, married and died close to their birthplace from Victorian times until World War II. A time when a way of life would recede into history, a lost world which older Sculcoates residents look back on with nostalgia.

In the 1930s the majority of Sculcoates children learned to swim in the warm water deposited into Barmston (Barmy) Drain by the power station. As children they played games together that varied according to the seasons, mostly in the streets as traffic was virtually non existent. After the children grew up to become householders, having played, attended school and then sometimes worked together led them to trust one another, as every house appeared to have the front door key hanging on a string dangling behind the letterbox, allowing anyone in need to enter the house. Remarkable occurrences, as such action would have disastrous consequences in today's world where nothing is safe from theft. An intriguing question without a ready answer being, why bother locking the door when everyone knows where the key is?

When interviewed residents memories were remarkable in as much as they all spoke about their past with the same voice. Despite the majority having little money to spend, they all expressed how they remembered with pleasure the community spirit of past times, which they claim no longer exists in today's more affluent society. No one recalled the noise from the factories, or smoke from the myriad of domestic and industrial chimneys that deposited soot all over the area. Perhaps with age there comes a time when the mind wears blinkers, unpleasantness is blanked out and only the good times are remembered.

1930s Wash days
Hands on History Museum 2007 - Hull

Night soil collection1920
G. Patrick

THE BRITISH GAS LIGHT COMPANY

On any cold winter morning in the 1940/50's the poor residents and ragged kids of the local area could be seen heading for the gas works in Bankside to collect the cheap coke for use as their household fuel. These works were erected in 1824 to supply coal gas to the Sculcoates people. Now, only tiny remains hint at the huge complex which once occupied this wasteland. Only windows in a wall and bricked up doors, now serving as a boundary next to the road, really show any evidence of its past. Inside the dispatch yard it was a scene like a 'Lowry' painting. Everything was black with coal dust and that awful gas smell filled the air. You paid your money at the little 'teller's' office and took your ticket to the man at the end of the big hoppers. He had a very large garden fork and an oversized pair of potato type scales, and he would weigh you your two or four stones of coke and tip it into your pram with probably an old tin bath or tea chest attached. The local coal merchants would be there filling their one hundredweight sacks and loading them on to their waiting horses and rullies.

These works were erected in 1824 to supply coal gas. The process had just been perfected to 'carbonate' coal, but they did not know how to store it.. If it was used it had to be burnt off, but in 1826 the gasometer was developed and made 'gas tight.'

The plant of 41 acres ran for 150 years and lasted until the advent of 'natural' North sea gas but now only the gasometers give a hint of its former use but it was always associated with smell, dirt and grime. It was self sufficient with an electric power station, a foundry, railway and a fire station and it supplied twenty square miles of the local area. The extraction of the gas for cheap domestic heating and street lighting also created the by-products of tar and creosote. It was built near the river because the process used 100,000 gallons of water a day and also barges could access direct from the coal fields of the West-Riding to the gates of the plant. Later in 1885 a rail connection was established from the Hull-Barnsley line at Fitzroy Street which then shared the deliveries.

The gasometers were huge landmarks and during the war they were always a vulnerable target for aircraft and Bankside was often holed and shells landed in the company's football and cricket field on Clough Road. The largest gasometer was hit in 1941 and exploded, the debris punctured the two smaller tanks either side of it. The tank there now is fairly modern and much bigger than the original ones and holds 'natural' gas. It became a daily routine to observe these tanks and it was in daily conversation. "If they are full there wont be an air-raid tonight – but if they were low- be prepared for a sleepless night." – did the Gas company have direct communications with Hitler?

HULL HYDRAULIC POWER COMPANY

Hull was the first town in the world to have a hydraulic power system for public use. The system was first envisaged and patented by Joseph Bramah in 1812 but had to wait for an advancement in technological capability before its realisation, by a man called Edward Baysand Ellington, in the 1870s.

The Hull system was seen as a prototype for the London Hydraulic Power Company and, eventually, companies in places as diverse as Glasgow and Buenos Aires.

The Hull Hydraulic Power Company was established, by an Act of Parliament, in 1872. The Act stated that the objective of the Company was to establish 'a system for applying power by hydraulic pressure to waterside and land cranes, used for the purpose of raising and lowering goods, and for working dock gates and other machinery'.

The power station was erected in 1875 and was situated on the corner of Machell Street and Catherine Street. It actually became operational in 1876 and, despite initial concerns about feasibility of the system, it proved successful. By 1895 it was supplying power to 58 machines and the total was up to 200 machines by c1900.

The system seemed to work as follows: water from the River Hull was pumped about 125 yards to the power station. A storage tank with filtering boxes covered the building and the water passed through this system and then onto steam driven pumping engines. It was then stored under a vertical ram, weighted with 57 tons of copper slag and sand, the housing of which stood 45 feet high when fully charged. This was called an accumulator (similar to a gasometer) and maintained the pressure. From the accumulator the pressurised water passed through the 6 inch mains pipes that ran along the River to Wellington Street/Humber Street to the south and Sculcoates Bridge to the north. The water used was metered at the consumer end and the excess water was then discharged back into the River Hull or the sewerage system. As the demand grew more and even bigger pumps were built in Machell Street and accumulators were developed in Grimsby Lane.

Hull's oil extracting industry thrived on the system and many new industries also benefited from hydraulic power. New businesses could tap into the hydraulic mains system to operate cranes, lifts, hoists, presses, bridges and dock gates and they no longer had to provide their own engines and pumps or relevant engineers. Buildings using hydraulic power could also easily adapt the system for fire fighting. Using simple apparatus it could easily be turned into a fire hydrant or sprinkler system. This attracted preferential insurance rates for the Companies using this feature. The Power Station and mains system suffered war damage in 1944 but did continue to operate until 1947. The company was wound up when Mr F.J. Haswell, the engineer and manager since 1904, retired.

A part of the building remain today, as does part of the tank, shown in the picture. Some mains pipes have been discovered in High Street and a number of inspection covers, bearing the initials HHPCO, can still be found.

Hull Hydraulic Power Company 2007
H & D LHRG

Hull Hydraulic Power Company inspection cover, Wincolmlee 2007
H & D LHRG

Blue Plaque 2007
H & D LHRG

SCULCOATES POWER STATION

Background

The supply of electricity came to Hull in the final quarter of the nineteenth century when the Hull Corporation was authorised to supply electric lighting in some of the streets in the Old Town and by 1882 the private company of Siemens was contracted to deliver the means of power for the undertaking. The experiment was short-lived however and was discontinued after two years, with Siemens unable to guarantee a reliable service. In 1890 the Corporation was given the necessary powers to generate and supply electricity and in 1893 an electricity generating station was opened in Dagger Lane for the purpose of supplying the Old Town. Initially 33 consumers took advantage of the new system but later that year the supply of electricity was extended to an area west of the Old Town and by 1894 there were 271 consumers.

In 1897 the horse-drawn tram system, which was operating on all of Hull's main roads, was becoming inefficient and in 1898 the Hull Corporation obtained powers to operate electric trams. During 1897-98 a temporary generating station was opened in North Street, with the number of consumers now rising to 960. In 1898 a new electricity generating station was opened in Sculcoates Lane on the western bank of the Barmston Drain on a 1.3 acre site that had been a former Corporation refuse depot, and prior to that, clay pits. The site had been originally purchased by the Corporation sanitary authorities in 1876 for waste disposal purposes. Sub-stations were opened in Argyle Street and Albion Street and during 1899-1900 11 miles of

electric tram lines had been laid and 65 trams purchased. At the end
of 1900 Hessle Road, Anlaby Road, Beverley Road, Holderness
Road and Spring Bank all had electric trams in service, connecting
the outlying areas to the town centre. As the tramway system was to
be a major user of electricity it was decided that it would have its
own supply and in 1899 a new power station was opened in
Osbourne Street for this purpose.

Sculcoates power station

The Sculcoates power station officially opened on 24 October 1898,
generating electricity by means of a 520 kilowatt reciprocating coal-
fired steam engine and fire-tube boilers. In 1899 the number of
consumers had risen to 2,267. On 6 August 1901 a piece of land
measuring almost 2 acres was purchased for power station extensions
and in 1904 a bridge was built over the Barmston Drain giving
railway access to new sidings for the movement of coal by rail,
which was to be delivered to the north side of the station by the Hull
and Barnsley Railway Company. On 12 August 1905 the last
delivery of coal carried by horse-drawn transport entered the power
station. The 1901 extension was to be the first of ten such extensions
carried out during the 20th century. In 1910 a further 7.1 acre piece
of land on the south side of Clough Road was purchased by the
Corporation from the Hull Estate Company Ltd, although only 2
acres related to the power station site. The station had by now
switched to the use of steam turbine generators and in 1914 the
annual plant capacity had risen to 11,800 kilowatts. Hull now had
4,415 consumers and by 1915 the supply area included Sutton and
Hessle. By 1922 ten parishes in Sculcoates Rural District Council

were supplied with electricity, many tramway routes in Hull had been extended, and it was now usual for newly-built houses to have electricity installed. All this led to an increase in consumers and by 1924 the total had risen to 9,470. At the same time the power station's capacity had risen to 24,340 kilowatts.

Meanwhile, by 1927 the Hull tramway system consisted of 21 miles of track using 180 tramcars and the demands made by the system were proving too great for the Osbourne Street generating station and it closed in 1930. The supply was then taken from the Sculcoates station where several wooden cooling towers, which had been constructed over the years, now totalled eight. These towers were not like the huge modern cooling towers but were about three times the height of an average house and were oblong in shape. The number of consumers had risen to 26,471 by 1930, an increase of 17,001 in six years. The Central Electricity Board had been created in 1926 and by 1930 a decision had been made to establish a National Grid for electricity generation, leading to Sculcoates power station operating as a 'selected generating station' in November 1931. By this time Hedon, Cottingham, parts of Beverley, Patrington, Sculcoates and Skirlaugh Rural District Councils had access to electricity supplies.

In 1935 the capacity of Sculcoates power station had risen to 52,000 kilowatts and was supplying power to 67,081 consumers. In 1939 the Central Electricity Generating Board began to take supplies from Sculcoates power station and 25% of all units generated were used in this way. The station now had an annual capacity of 97,000 kilowatts while supplying 95,735 consumers.

During the years of World War Two the power station must have been a prime target for German bombers and documentary and photographic evidence obtained from German archives in the post-war years confirmed this, yet surprisingly, the power station suffered very little damage. During the course of the air assault some 25 high explosive bombs fell within half a mile of the power station and eight within 200 yards of the engine rooms. In every one of the eighty raids on Hull electricity cables were cut and equipment in many factories and homes were damaged or destroyed, but the power station escaped relatively unscathed and breaks in the supply system were usually quickly restored to customers.

Immediately after the war work began on the construction of a new 300-feet high concrete cooling tower that soon became a familiar landmark on the Hull landscape after it opened on 7 December 1946. Shortly afterwards the power station was involved in an exchange of 3 acres of their land with a piece of the same size belonging to Needler's Ltd, with Needlers using their portion for recreational purposes. Power was now being supplied to an area of over 160 square miles with some output going to the South East Yorkshire Light and Power Company which supplied a large part of the East Riding. 1947 saw the electricity industry nationalised and the following year the British Electricity Board, along with 14 area Boards, were established. The whole of Hull's supply now came under the Yorkshire Electricity Board. The power station was now manned by a staff of 213 and its annual capacity was 124.000 kilowatts. Power was now supplied to 101,500 consumers.

The beginning of the end

During the 1950s and 1960s the ever growing demands for electricity, combined with the need to create less pollution, led to a gradual run-down of coal-fired power stations with oil, nuclear power, and eventually natural and North Sea gas being used for the generation of electricity. Sculcoates power station had nearly passed its sell-by date and by 1964 was working on a reduced capacity of 122,000 kilowatts, which was slightly lower than previously. The staff total had by that time risen to 240.

Sculcoates power station ceased generating electricity in 1976 with the number of employees down to 98 on 1 June 1976 and the demolition of the site began in early 1979, with the whole site cleared by 1981. The area remained dormant until 1992 when the Hull Corporation purchased the site from National Power for £100,000. After further clearance work including the removal of the immense reinforced concrete foundations of the former power station, during which the modern civil engineers paid fulsome tribute to their Victorian forefathers, the site was made level and safe. It is now being redeveloped for private housing.

Sculcoates Power Station 1950
Chris Ketchell Collection

SCULCOATES TANNERY

'Mostly they worked in the tan yards or the paint factory, menial tasks, low wages.......

...even after the war they were lucky to be getting £3 a week...they worked hard and a lot used to go for a drink in the morning at the Golden Ball ' (A local resident of Sculcoates)

The name of Holmes has been associated with the tanning of hides since the early nineteenth century and still exists today as ' Holmes Halls Tanners' in Wincolmlee/Air Street.

Tanning is a process whereby animal skins are turned into leather to be used in The manufacture of such items as clothing, shoes, upholstery, saddlery, and at one time, in machinery for drive belts and hinges. Tanning has never been one of Hull's major industries if judged by the number of tanneries. There is also a lack of street names to act as reminders of past tanneries although at one time Waterhouse Lane was known as Tan House Lane.

At the be ginnin gof the nineteenth centur ya tanner named John Holmes came to Hull from Doncaster and began working in Church Street (now Wincolmlee) in 1803. He later opened tanneries on Anlaby Road and by the middle of the century the Holmes family had become the main Hull tanners. By the end of the century Thos. Holmes and Sons were the only tanners in Hull and operated from Anlaby Road, Campbell Street, Church Street and Providence Row. At one time 500 people were employed by the Wincolmlee/Air Street factory although today's workforce is a tenth of that number

'Me mam had a little shop on the corner of Bournemouth Street and she used to bake for the factories round, Needlers, Sangwins, the tan yard and everywhere......I used to get up at six o'clock every morning to help her do it'. (A local resident remembering the war period)

Animal skins if untreated would rot and quickly become unusable. Tanning is designed to prevent this happening. The process first involves the removal of the inner layer of flesh (fat) together with the outer layer of hair and then the central layer of fibres (collagen) has to be stabilised or 'tanned' to prevent putrefaction. This middle layer, about one centimetre thick, has then become leather and can be split to produce material of different thicknesses for different applications.

The tanning process has been practised throughout history initially using chemicals containing tannic acid and made from vegetable matter. The process could take many months or even years to produce the finished material. Fortunately in more recent times tanning can be achieved in a matter of hours using salts of chromium. This latter method leaves the leather stiff and hard and coloured blue. The leather will later be further treated to make it soft, pliable and coloured and turned into leather goods. (Pallets of 'wet blues' waiting to be exported can be seen when passing the Air Street entrance of the tannery today)

The nature of the dirty hides with their attached layers of fat and dirty hair and the chemicals used always ensured that the tanning process was a smelly affair. Air Street however, which runs alongside the present tannery, was not named because of the odours

63

emanating from the tannery but apparently because of its once 'open airy situation'!

'......Oh the tannery! You haven't lived until you've smelled that.'

(a former Sculcoates resident)

Tannery building from the River Hull
Holmes Hall Tanners

Advertisement for bends (hides)
Holmes Hall Tanners

SISSONS OF HULL

Among the many industries that lined Bankside in this particular area of Sculcoates was the paint industry, and specifically one company that being Sissons Brothers & Co.

When people look back they remember a company such as Sissons Brothers being on the original site where the company first started trading. Thomas Sissons, then trading as Sissons, Weddle & Co, founded the company in 1803 in conjunction with John Weddle. The premises were on the east bank of the River Hull in the Lime Street and Grove area, making not only oil and paint, but also mustard, French and pearl barley.

In 1804 they took over a number of properties in Witham including the mill and warehouse of Joseph Wilkinson. The involvement with John Weddle lasted into the 1820s.

By 1826 the company had become Sissons & Co and were still based in the Groves making paint colour, Stone Blue, mustard, pearl barley, and also whiting. Between 1826 and 1831 they moved to Bankside in the Sculcoates district and were then trading as Sissons Brothers & Co.

Over the course of the nineteenth and twentieth centuries they developed this site covering a total of twenty acres. As with most industrial premises in the Bankside area of Hull the site of Sissons Brothers & Co suffered bomb damage during the course of World War 2.

In 1956 Sissons joined the Reckitt and Colman group and was later sold to Donald Macpherson and Co of Bury, and the site was later closed. This bringing to an end a total of 153 years of trading under the Sissons name. Where the factory once was is now derelict land.

Sissons gate piers 2007
H & D LHRG

SCHOOLDAYS IN SCULCOATES

The parish of Sculcoates has had many schools over the years, some still in use while others have been demolished and are just a memory. Probably the school that concerned most of the children who grew up in the Sculcoates Lane area, and certainly the most prominent in the district was Stepney Lane School, known locally as Beverley Road School. This school was opened in 1886 and was designed to accommodate 700 mixed pupils. The school motto was 'Labour to learn before you grow old, for learning's more precious than silver or gold'. The architect who designed the school was Mr. William Botterill and the building contractor was Mr. J. Skinner. The building was of red brick and Ancaster stone with a roof of red tiles surmounted in the centre with a turret which was not only a pretty ornament but also useful for ventilation. Hot water pipes, fitted by King and Company of Holy Trinity South Church Side, provided a central heating system. A cookery and kitchen with a small scullery was attached to the double-storey block and all the rooms were given a dado of white glazed bricks, as the value of cleanliness with the large numbers of children involved was not overlooked. An eighty year old lady who attended the Girl's Senior School remembered that the girl's school was on the first floor and as the girls came down the fire escape at playtime they would wave to the boys in the ground floor class rooms. One gentleman recalled the use of corporal punishment by being caned on the hand. The boys sometimes pulled their hand away but the teachers would bring the cane back up and catch them on the back of the hand which was often more painful.

He remembered the school swimming teams that dominated the Hull Schools' Swimming Galas during the 1930s. The school won a lot of trophies and medals and it was often said that it was because of the amount of swimming the pupils did in Barmston Drain. This was confirmed by another resident who said the drain was popular because the water was always warm due to the recycling of water between the drain and Sculcoates Power Station that was on the side of the drain. Another lady resident remarked that the girls would never swim in the drain but she clearly remembers the famous Hull international swimmer Jack Hale swimming there as a boy. She went on to say that Jack lived in Fleet Street and when he swam for England in the 1948 London Olympic Games a bus was organised to take his friends and neighbours to see him swim at the old Empire Pool, Wembley. In 1969 the school was renamed Stepney Primary School and celebrated its centenary in 1986. Today, in 2007, the school is still in use and is earning a wonderful reputation for being one of best top ten percent primary schools in the country.

Other schools in Sculcoates

Sculcoates parish was incorporated into the Parliamentary Borough of Hull in 1837 but prior to that there were already two schools operating in the parish. The first of these was the old Sculcoates Subscription (later National) School that was opened by public subscription in 1804. This school was next to the parish workhouse in Carr Street, replacing an earlier one of 1787. It was re-organised as a National School in 1818 and in 1838 had 170 boys and 60 girls enrolled. The school closed in 1849. The other one was the

Sculcoates Girls School situated in Oxford Street that dated from 1834. Both of these schools passed into the parish of St. Paul's in 1844 and consequently another parish school near St. Mary's Church was opened in Bankside in 1852, mainly through the efforts of T.S. Bonnin, curate-in-charge.

Sculcoates Girls School in Oxford Street was one of Hull's first schools to be built with Government aid. It also served as a Mission Church until St. Paul's was built in 1844. Thereafter it housed St. Paul's Girls School until 1872 when a new building for girls and infants was added to Sculcoates St. Paul's National School.

Sculcoates St. Mary's School was erected in 1852 in Bankside, replacing Sculcoates National School and Sculcoates Girls School, which had both passed into the new St. Paul's parish in 1844. The school was built to accommodate 150 boys and girls but the attendance was 296 in 1872 and 257 in 1894 with 244 attending in 1904. The school was a single-storied structure of red brick with white brick ornamentation and originally had a small bellcote on the front gable end. Shortly after its opening the school was honoured by a visit from Mr. Samuel Wilderspin who was a founder of the Infant School Movement in 1824. The site was later transferred to the Local Education Authority and closed in 1904. The building is still standing on the edge of the River Hull along Bankside.

Sculcoates St. Pauls National School opened in 1858 as a boys school, supplementing the Sculcoates Girls School taken over by the parish in 1844. A girls infants school was added in 1872 increasing places to 722. These grew to 878 by 1897 making this Hull's second largest voluntary school but were later reduced to 790, comprising 336 boys, 212 girls and 242 infants. In 1922 it was transferred to the Local Education Authority and in 1925 was reorganised for 336 girls and 389 combined juniors and infants. Average attendance in 1938 was 419. The school closed in 1940.

Board Schools in Sculcoates

The Kingston upon Hull School Board was constituted under an Act of Parliament in 1871. During its short life 1870-1902 the Hull School Board built some 37 schools, several of which were in Sculcoates, including the ones mentioned below.

Park Road School was built in 1872 for 750 mixed pupils and was originally the parish school of All Saints Church before being taken over by the Hull Board in 1876. It was demolished in 1990 and is now the site of Friary Close flats.

Lincoln Street Board School was built in 1874 for 816 mixed pupils. It was demolished in 1997 and for the last few years of its existence was used as an annexe of the University of Lincolnshire and Humberside.

Fountain Road Board School was built in 1877 for 795 mixed pupils. It closed after 1963 and was used as the Kingston Community Centre before being demolished in 1981.

Northumberland Avenue Board School was also built in 1897 to accommodate 700 mixed pupils and was enlarged in 1900 by a further 300 places. The school closed in 1942 before becoming a special school and is now in use partly by the Humber Archaeology Partnership and partly as an industrial store. The separate block, which is now Fountain House, was built in 1904 and was the first by the City Architect Mr. J.H.Hirst.

Blundell Street Board School was built in 1878 and was designed to accommodate 750 mixed pupils. It eventually became the Hull School of Architecture before being taken over by the University of Lincolnshire and Humberside as its Students Union, being called The Strand. It closed in 1998, was set on fire in May 1999 and despite various planning applications for the University to have it demolished being refused it is still standing although severely damaged. It is currently the oldest surviving Board School in Hull and is listed Grade II by the Department of National Heritage as being of Special Architectural or Historic interest.

Clifton Street Board School was built in 1892 and is still in existence as Clifton Primary School.

Brunswick Avenue Board School was built in 1891 to accommodate 650 senior boys and 520 senior girls and was the Hull School Board's first Higher Grade School. In 1992 it became Brunswick House, the Humberside County Council's social services headquarters, and is now the Hull City Council's social services and leisure services offices. The building is also listed Grade II by the Department of National Heritage as being of Special Architectural or Historic interest.

No doubt many residents of Sculcoates will have happy memories of some of these schools and it is good to see that a few of these fine old Victorian buildings still have a function in the modern world.

Beverley Road School 2007
H & D LHRG

CHARTERHOUSE LANE SCHOOL

Before the 1870s, elementary education was provided by the non-conformists and, largely, the Anglicans: school attendance was often irregular and places insufficient. Forster's Elementary Education Act, 1870, was designed to fill the gap in provision, and so began 'state' education. Local, elected School Boards built and financed these new schools: Charterhouse Lane is an excellent example of the type and is a grade II listed building within the Charterhouse Conservation Area. Stand in Charterhouse Lane, opposite what was the girls' entrance, and examine the school buildings: the style, with its circular windows, its turrets and towers is Gothic Revival and, architecturally, the school is regarded as one of the best Victorian buildings in Hull. On the wall of the single-storey building opposite, chiselled in masonry, is the evidence for when it was built -1881; its purpose - a Board School; and, symbolically , who owned it - the ratepayers of Kingston-upon-Hull, hence the three crowns shield. This building was the infants' department for 243 children. The main block was for 251 boys on the ground floor, and 251 girls on the first floor. The evidence for this arrangement is clearly spelled out: 'BOYS' above the Wincolmlee entrance to the yard and above the east doorway into the main building, 'GIRLS' above the doorway to the first floor on the north side.

 The pupils were well ordered, as evidenced by the girls' stairs to the first floor. The children were required to walk up on the left and down on the other side. Walking up creates more friction and wear, and this can still be seen (despite some 1980s reconstructive infill) on the steps today. The rule was obeyed! Punctuality was a virtue: hence, the bell was tolled to call the children to school. The bell tower still exists on the main building; however, when it was made safe in the 1980s, the bell was removed and is now in the Guildhall. A decent education required good attendance, so Certificates of Regular Attendance, Third Class, Second Class and First Class, were given. In 1905, infant pupil George Edge received only a Second Class Certificate because he missed just one day's schooling! The stick was used, but so was the 'carrot' in promoting school values and ethos.

The accommodation remained unchanged until the late-1960s, and the outdoor toilets remained after that! The main block comprised, on each floor, three permanent rooms, plus two large areas each of which could be made into classrooms using floor to ceiling movable partitions which, thanks to robust Victorian standards of workmanship, still worked in the 1980s. The infants had two permanent classrooms and one large area which could be divided. So it was quite a large school. But, built for 745 pupils (1881), by 1904 average attendance was 676, and by 1938 only 392. Subsidised housing on the big new '20s and '30s green-field council estates, then wartime evacuation depleted child numbers locally.

However the buildings were given a new lease of life towards the end of World War II. Estcourt Street School, Newbridge Road, was destroyed by bombing in 1941. The Seniors (comprising girls specialising in commercial subjects), at first dispersed, were soon accommodated at Flinton Grove School, then later occupied

Charterhouse Lane. Because they only had a concrete yard, The Master of The Charterhouse allowed the girls access to his gardens. In 1949, new premises in Hopewell Road were completed for Estcourt High, releasing scarce accommodation in these post-war years at Charterhouse Lane. In 1950, nearby Lincoln Street was designated an all-girls school and the Senior boys were transferred to Charterhouse Lane; a new secondary modern, Charterhouse High School was born. However, in 1963, it had only 150 pupils. The policy of 'bigger schools are better schools' brought an end to school provision at Charterhouse Lane.

In 1967, the building became an annexe of Hull College of Technology: the future of this educational, architectural and historical gem now seemed secure. The Queen's Gardens campus had opened in 1956, initially for technical training courses. Despite further building on the site, it was never big enough for expanding needs. Consequently, further education largely grew by taking over redundant Board school buildings. When the 'Tech' closed in 1976, and the reformulated College of Further Education opened, 10 old Board Schools were in use, including Charterhouse Lane Annexe. Its proximity to the main site gave it a significant role: it often buzzed with activity, full to capacity: and for some years the former infants' building was the Hull College Nursery.

But in 2007, after 40 years as a college annexe, with the enormous College building programme in recent years, especially around the main campus, the Charterhouse Lane site has become outdated, redundant and is to be sold. How secure is its future now?

Charterhouse School
H & D LHRG

Charterhouse School
H & D LHRG

HOSTELRIES

It would be totally remiss when recording any sort of history of Sculcoates not to include a few brief notes on some of the many hostelries to be found in the area both past and present.

Sculcoates being for the most part an industrial area with a lot of working class folk living in the numerous streets was always going to have several pubs within its boundaries. It would be impossible to cover all the many inns and taverns in this article so we will just detail some of the more famous ones.

We must start with the inn, which took its name from the area itself, the Sculcoates Arms, known locally as the 'Scully Arms'. This hostelry was situated on Charles Street at the corner of Raywell Street. This pub stood out due to its attractive exterior.

It was built in c1845 and was originally listed as 'beer house'. It was first shown on the 1853 Ordnance Survey plans when it was marked as the Sculcoates Inn. The famous ceramic tiled exterior was added when the building was refurbished in the latter part of the 19th century. It is clear looking at the pictures of the pub that David Reynard Robinson, the Hull master builder who was famous for this distinctive style, was involved in the façade of the building.

The bar, which contained eye-catching white glazed tiles was not accessible to the fairer sex who had to sit in the snug, which was entered through a side door from Raywell Street. It was run for a long time by a Joseph Gorman and was known locally as 'Smokey Joe's' after the said gentleman.

The Sculcoates Arms finally closed its doors for business on Sunday 9th April 1972. This proved to be a very traumatic night not only for the regulars of this traditional old pub but also to its many patrons of other hostelries in Hull who made an emotional return visit for the 'Scully' Arms' final night.

The building was demolished in the latter part of 1983 but not before two local historians, Roy Dresser and Christopher Ketchell, managed to recover some of the glazed bricks and stained glass windows.

The second pub to mention is the Golden Ball which was situated on the northern side of Air Street to the west of the graveyard of the old St. Mary's Church. It was much used by the workers of the tannery of Thomas Holmes, which is now known as Holmes Hall Tannery. The inn was originally called the Blue Ball and stood alone in a little terrace by the name of Eliza's Row. It was first listed as the Golden Ball in 1882 and ten years later was purchased by the Hull Brewery Co. The pub was always a busy hostelry set as it was in a thriving industrial area and its customers were a mix of factory workers and the people who lived in the area and used it as their local.

The Golden Ball finally called last orders on Saturday 15th June 1996, which like the final night of the Sculcoates Arms, was an emotional evening. The inn was full of locals, people coming back to the area for the Golden Ball's last night and the members of CAMRA who had been involved in a long fight to save the Golden Ball unfortunately without success. This pub was one of three hostelries in Air Street at one time the other two being the Tanners Arms and the Horse Clippers Arms.

The Horse Clippers Arms was certainly the more famous of the other two situated as it was almost directly opposite the Golden Ball. This hostelry was originally built as a dwelling house in the 1840s, and had become a 'beer house' by 1862. Two years later the resident of the premises a certain Thomas Kelswick was listed as a 'horse clipper'. A further couple of years on this same Thomas Kelswick was recorded as the victualler of the Horse Clippers Arms. This like many pubs was named after an industry in the area. The Horse Clippers Arms closed for business in 1936 although the building remained and suffered extensive bomb damage during the course of the Second World War. The derelict buildings were finally demolished in the 1950s.

The majority of the pubs in the industrial area of Sculcoates however were to be found in Wincomlee. One current hostelry, which is still very popular, is the Bay Horse on the western side of Wincomlee on the corner of Machell Street. This inn dates back to the very early part of the 19th century first being named around 1802. Richardson, Terrington & Co owned it in 1806, and one of the first recorded victuallers was William Smith.

Peter Robson rebuilt the pub in 1878 and the Bay Horse like many properties in Hull suffered from bomb damage in 1943 although this was reported at the time to be only minor. A wall between the bar and the smoke room was demolished in 1960. The pub has always had a Rugby League connection and numerous excellent photographs of local teams, both Hull Kingston Rovers and Hull, adorned the walls. Len Casey, a famous player with both clubs and a Great

Britain international, was mine host there between 1982 and 1985. Standing not 100 yards from the Bay Horse is the Whalebone. This is a timely reminder of the whaling industry which took place in the area many years ago. It originally had its address in Church Street and was first listed in 1814 as being 8 Church Street, this under the title of the Splaw Bone. The first record found of it being listed as Wincomlee was in 1892 when it was situated at number 165. Church Street appears to have been incorporated into Wincomlee c1890.

Another famous tavern on Wincomlee was the Old Greenland Fishery Inn. This hostelry was converted from housing in the 1820s and by 1823 was trading under the title of the Greenland Fishery under the stewardship of James Robinson when it was listed as being number 27 Church Street this being north of its junction with York Street. Again its title gives reference to the whaling industry and the ships which sailed from the shipyards in the district. This pub actually closed for business in 1933 when the licence was transferred to the Endike Hotel in Endike Lane.

The De La Pole Tavern once stood at the eastern end of Charterhouse Lane at its junction with Wincomlee. It was originally a beer house called the Jug, but following the widening of Wincomlee in the middle of the 19th century it was rebuilt and named the De La Pole Tavern. The earliest record of this hostelry was in 1846 when it was situated at 1 Wincomlee. The Hull Brewery eventually took over the business in 1924 and continued to run the inn until it was finally closed in 1933 and the premises were later demolished.

We must also mention the Ferryboat Tavern on Wincomlee, which was originally a row of houses on the eastern side of Wincomlee to the south of the Sculcoates bridge. It was originally a beerhouse and became known as the Ferryboat Tavern in the 1840s. Around c1870 it was known for a time as Tiger No.5 due to the fact that a John Stephenson had purchased several pubs and given them all the name Tiger with a number. This however was a short- lived idea and the hostelry soon reverted back to the Ferryboat Tavern.

The Ferryboat Inn or Tavern, it was known by both titles, continued trading until the late 1930s until it finally closed its doors on the 17th December 1936 and was later demolished. The victualler at the time of its closing was Joseph Atkin Wardlow.

One little inn that still exists today is the Kingston which is on the eastern side of Cumberland Street, and which has been open for business for over 150 years. The first recorded landlord is J. Plant who was mine host in 1851. It is still much used today by the people who work in the area.

Another 'lost pub' that deserves a mention is the much-loved Burns Head on Waterloo Street, which was situated at its southern end with its junction with Richmond Terrace, now no longer in existence. It was built in the middle of the 19th century and like many other hostelries was originally only a beerhouse. If you look at the census of 1851 you will note that it is listed as Burns Head. In 1890 it was expanded to include the property next door. By the 1920s the original beerhouse façade had disappeared and had been replaced by a Mock Tudor black and white frontage. This inn was demolished under compulsory purchase in 1972.

This has been a taste of some of the pubs both past and present within the boundaries of Sculcoates and this is without touching any of the many hostelries on Beverley Road.

The Golden Ball
Paul Gibson

The Sculcoates Arms
Paul Gibson

NATIONAL PICTURE THEATRE

On 23rd December 1914, some four months after England had declared war on Germany the National Picture Theatre opened its doors to the public. The cinema was comparatively narrow to its length, being approximately 15 metres by 62 metres, designed by architects Runton and Barry who also worked on the Garden Village development for Reckitt's.

Contemporary accounts claimed the National's decorations to be elegant and stylish, the new cinema aimed to be the most comfortable in Hull stating that sitting in its plush softly upholstered seats was like being sat in a father's cosy armchair at home.

When the National was built in the silent cinema days a piano usually provided the accompaniment, this was not so at Hull's latest cinema it was more upmarket, provision had been made for an orchestra to accompany silent films before sound track arrived. After surviving the 1914-1918 Great War, fate decreed that the National Cinema would not repeat this feat in World War II, as on the 18th March 1941 the cinema would show its last film. Somewhat ironically as it happened, as this was Charlie Chaplin's The Great Dictator, a satire on Adolf Hitler's rise to power. The Fuhrer's airforce, the Luftwaffe must have taken umbrage at this as they dropped a bomb which exploded, probably in the car park behind the rear wall at 9.50 pm, 10 minutes before all cinemas closed in wartime.

A report given by the manager in the Hull Daily Mail said there were about 150 people sheltering in the foyer with a few others in the rear stalls. After the bomb dropped the manager said it was remarkable how well every one behaved, there was no panic and no one received a scratch. No doubt the bombs timing would have been crucial in avoiding injury to the cinemagoers, as in those days the programme ended with the National Anthem being played, an event which signalled a rush for the exits to avoid standing to attention. The projectionist claimed he switched off the heating and electricity supplies after the national anthem had been played, suggesting a measured response to the bomb damage. The manager added that the foreman had just returned from attending the boiler at the rear of the cinema when the back wall and the screen were blown in. When there was a lull in the bombing the manager then conducted all the patrons to the safety of a private bomb shelter next door. Over the years several claims have been made about casualties, the last one in the Hull Daily Mail on February 20th 2007 going as far as to claim people were killed in the cinema and it is believed bodies are still there on its site. There is nothing in the reports made at the time to suggest that when the bomb fell, other than an orderly evacuation of all patrons took place. Furthermore, there is no entry in the Hull City Council World War II documentation that recorded the deaths of any Hull citizens caused by enemy action. While it is accepted that records are not infallible, they are another source confirming that there were no deaths when the National Cinema sustained bomb damage during a World War II air raid on 18th March 1941.

Conflicting reports, some made many years after the event illustrate the problems historians can face when attempting to record an accurate portrayal of an event, unless someone can substantiate these varying statements, such as finding human remains on site. Until evidence like this is forthcoming, the contemporary reports made at the time when the event occurred have to be accepted as what happened.

Now the National's façade is partly hidden by an advertising hoarding, above it four Ionic pilasters can be seen which once supported a large pediment that has been removed in the 1960s for safety reasons. Various plants and trees have become established in the auditorium, one bush has managed to establish itself at the top of the façade and appears to be flourishing. Now that plant life has gained a foothold on the buildings remains, shows that nature is taking an interest in the building, perhaps more of Hull's citizens will now do the same, as the National Picture Theatre remains have been officially recognised. Having been awarded a Grade II listing after a campaign by the National Civilian World War II Memorial Trust it may be the last surviving example of a civilian building damaged in the blitz. The adjacent Swan Inn, which has passed unscathed through two world wars, does not appear that it is going to survive long into the twenty first century. The inn now bears more than a passing resemblance to its bomb damaged neighbour, slates are falling off, allowing rain water ingress to damage the interior fabric, floor boards are missing and debris is scattered all over the building adding to the air of desolation. Should the Swan Inn continue to deteriorate at its present rate, it would make the building an inappropriate neighbour for the National's future development.

Over the years various suggestions have been made about the damaged cinema, one being on Monday June 26th 2000. A Yorkshire Post newspaper reporter's article discussed the site's future with the Hull historian who was campaigning for the cinema's war damaged site to be listed. Perhaps the idea made then can be adopted in some way, namely that Hull having been more heavily bombed city per capita in the country during World War II. A fitting memorial to commemorate this fact would be to incorporate what is left of the façade and site into a peace garden, by doing this it would turn the National's remains into a permanent memorial; a fitting tribute for a bombsite that time forgot.

National Picture Theatre after air raid, March 1941
Courtesy of Hull City Archives

National Picture Theatre 2007
H & D LHRG

88

SCULCOATES WORKHOUSE

Background – The Poor Law Acts

Care of the poor, or poor relief, as it came to be known, has been an on-going problem since medieval times. As early as 1388 attempts were made to control vagrancy. The Roman Catholic Church was England's religious body at the time and the Church did what it could to help those in need. After the suppression of the monasteries in 1535-6 the responsibility was passed on to the parishes and in 1563 the first Poor Law Act was passed, and churchwardens were appointed to gather and collect the means of supporting paupers. The Poor Law Act of 1601 was to be the basis of poor law administration for two centuries. The Act divided the poor receiving relief into three general categories; The able-bodied who were to be found work, the impotent, or physically unfit for work, and people who were too old to work and who may have been homeless. Parishes were allowed to levy a rate and from this some poorhouses were built, but in the majority of cases parish workhouses were just ordinary houses used for the purpose. Certain prominent people in the parish were appointed Overseers of the Poor and were authorised to collect the poor rate. Various amendments were made to the act over the years but the act remained in force until 1834.

The following description taken from White's Directory of Hull for 1826 shows briefly how an Old Poor Law workhouse was administered, how many paupers were received and what it cost to keep them;

'Sculcoates Workhouse

Situated in Wilson's Row, Wincolmlee, is under the direction of a visitor and four guardians, the affairs of this asylum for the destitute poor are managed by Mr. John Fleming, the present Governor. From 4 April 1825 to 27 March 1826 the weekly average of paupers in this house was 59, and the average expense of the food of each pauper was 3/2d (0-16p) per week. The Matron was Mrs Hannah Fleming.'
It is not known if the workhouse was one large house, a combination of consecutive smaller houses, or perhaps a converted much larger building.

There are records of just two poor law parish workhouses in the Sculcoates area, the one in Wilson's Row and later another one was situated in Carr Street, which ran between Green Lane and Scott Street. Scott Street had a junction with Wilson's Row and the two workhouses would have been in very close proximity. The Carr Lane workhouse was the one that was in use in the final few years prior to the opening of the new Sculcoates Union Workhouse on Beverley Road.

The Poor Law Amendment Act of 1834, or the New Poor Law Act as it came to be known, caused major changes to be made in poor relief. It minimised the provision of outdoor relief and made confinement in a workhouse the central element of the new system. No outdoor relief was to be paid and admission to a workhouse for the impotent and helpless poor was to be the last resort for paupers. Workhouse administrators were encouraged to make life in them as unpleasant as possible in an effort to deter people from seeking relief. Married couples were to be separated and children taken from their parents, communication between them was not allowed in communal places such as chapel and refectory, and only infrequent reunions were permitted.

The Poor Law was administered by three Poor Law Commissioners who employed Assistant Commissioners for local inspections. Parishes were encouraged to form unions to enable the provision of large union workhouses, of which Sculcoates was one, and Boards of Guardians were appointed to manage poor relief in the parish. In 1913 a Union Workhouse was officially retitled a 'Poor Law Institution', and indoor relief was increasingly confined to the extremely poor. The National Insurance Act of 1911 began the provision of social insurance that eventually led to the modern benefit system started in 1946. Finally, the Local Government Act of 1929 saw the powers of the Boards of Guardians abolished, as was the term 'pauper', and the powers were transferred to the local authorities who were encouraged to turn Institutions into Hospitals. This is what happened to the Beverley Road Institution.

The Sculcoates Poor Law Union

The Sculcoates Poor Law Union was formed on 6 July 1837 and the controlling power was in the hands of an elected Board of Guardians consisting of twenty-seven members. Eighteen local parishes comprised the new union and included the eastern and northern areas of Hull and rural areas to the east and west of the town. The eighteen parishes listed below were represented by the twenty-seven members and the larger parishes with more than one member are shown in brackets;

Anlaby, Cottingham (2), Drypool (2), Kirkella, Westella, North Ferriby, Hedon (2), Hessle, Marfleet, Melton, Preston, Sculcoates (4), Southcoates (2), Sutton and Stoneferry (2), Swanland, Waudby, Welton, and Willerby (2).

The population falling within the Sculcoates Poor Law Union at the 1831 census had been 29,238 with parishes ranging in size from Waudby, with a population of 50, to Sculcoates itself, with a population of 13,486. The average annual poor-rate expenditure for the period 1834-36 had been £11,407, or 8/10d per head of the population.

The New Sculcoates Workhouse

The new workhouse was built in 1844 at the corner of Beverley Road and Fountain Road to a design by Mr. H.F. Lockwood who designed many fine buildings in Hull. In J.J. Sheahan's 'History of Kingston upon Hull' the building is described as follows;

'The workhouse is a large handsome red brick structure, with stone dressings, chiefly in the Tudor style of architecture, erected in 1844, at the expense of about £11,000, affording accommodation for 500 paupers. The front range of the edifice, which is about 370 feet wide, is the most ornamental, and consists of a central tower in which is a clock, the board room, and at the ends are the receiving wards. Behind these, the central or principal range of building is about 200 feet in length and three storeys high; behind these are the kitchens and other offices; then comes the large dining-hall, which has a pulpit at the end of it as it also serves as a chapel; and behind this is a large kitchen garden. There are several courts or airing-yards and the whole area occupies about four and a half acres. During the past year (1863) the average number of in-door paupers was 290 and the cost of their maintenance was £4,879. The workhouse also had a hospital along with wash-houses, tailors' and shoe-makers' shops and school rooms. In 1864 the Chairman of the Board of Guardians was Mr. Daniel Sykes Esq., of Kirkella, the workhouse Master was Mr. Joseph Rowland Jessop and Mrs. Emma Jessop was the Matron.

It is interesting to note that the Hull Advertiser described the building in typical Victorian fashion, writing that 'the beautiful immense structure … its front aspect would not disgrace the residence of a nobleman.' Later it writes 'the spacious and airy rooms of the paupers command a prospect that would be envied by many of our inhabitants residing in the town.' It finishes by saying 'It is of great beauty and has a far more noble appearance than any of the fine edifices in the locality.' Fine words indeed but later comments are not so flattering. Although Brown's 'Illustrated Guide to Hull' (1891) calls it 'a handsome building in the Elizabethan style', Pevsner and Neave in 1995 describes 'the gaunt three-storey brick buildings but with a pretty Gothic clock tower.' Ian Goldthorpe in his book of 2005 uses the terms 'the worst design Lockwood ever carried out in Hull' … 'buildings coarsely detailed' and 'the gables on the wings … clumsily and coarsely created.'

Life in a Workhouse

What was life like in a typical Victorian workhouse? Each day the paupers would rise early and assemble for prayers and roll call, after which they would take breakfast, which like all meals, was eaten in silence and in separate dining rooms. During the day the men would be employed, often on such hated tasks like oakum picking, bone-crushing and breaking stones. Oakum picking meant untwisting lengths of old rope and picking the fibres apart. The fibres were then sold and spun again for use in ropes or cheap mats. The women were employed in 'household work', usually in the tailors' shops or in the wash-houses which all workhouses had. Children were supposed to have at least three hours daily schooling 'in reading, writing, and in the other principles of the Christian religion.'

All paupers were clothed in the official workhouse dress. During the day the paupers would be given dinner, and later on, supper. The day would end with prayers and all had to be in bed by 9-00pm when the Master and Matron would visit the wards to ensure that all fires and lights were extinguished. The food given to paupers was strictly regulated in an attempt to make the diet below the standard of food that the lowest paid independent labourer would expect to eat. The diet was very basic and very monotonous and meat was only served once a week. Any pauper could quit the workhouse upon giving the Master three hours notice of his wish to do so, but a man with a family could only leave if he took his family with him. But as anyone who was in a workhouse was very unlikely to be given a job enabling them to be in a position to leave, this would have been the exception rather than the rule. Finally, no one could visit a pauper in the workhouse without permission from the Master, and even then the visit had to take place in the presence of the Master or Matron. The following is an example of a diet sheet for able-bodied men in the Stow Union Workhouse in Suffolk;

- Breakfast, every day of the week – seven ounces of bread and one and a half pints of gruel.
- Dinner, for five days of the week - eight ounces of bread and one ounce of cheese.

  for one day of the week - one pound of meat pudding and vegetables.

  for one day of the week – one pound of suet pudding and vegetables.
- Supper, for every day of the week – seven ounces of bread and one ounce of cheese.

The ration for able-bodied women was five ounces of bread and twelve ounces of pudding. Gruel was oatmeal boiled in milk or water. Old people of sixty and over were allowed one ounce of tea, five ounces of butter and seven ounces of sugar instead of receiving gruel. Christmas time was slightly better for the paupers as local dignitaries and businessmen would contribute seasonal fare to the workhouse. As far as Sculcoates Workhouse is concerned, J.J. Sheahan records 'that for the Christmas of 1862 Mr. William

Lonsdale, confectioner of Adelaide Street, Hull, presented an immense pork pie which weighed one hundred and forty pounds along with one hundred pork pies weighing half a pound each. The small pies were for the children and the larger one for the adult inmates of the workhouse'. Mr. Clarke Butlin made a gift of one hundred cheesecakes. Other donations included money, books and other such seasonal items.

More of Sculcoates Workhouse

The growth of the pauper population of the workhouse in the second half of the nineteenth century can be shown from the official census figures for the period;

  1851 Male paupers 142, female paupers 107, total 249.

  1861 Male paupers 125, female paupers 118, total 243.

  1871 Male paupers 158, female paupers 141, total 299 plus 3 vagrants.

  1881 Figures not available. Workhouse could accommodate 620 paupers.

  1891 Male paupers 265, female paupers 202, total 467 plus 10 vagrants.

  1901 Male paupers 402, female paupers 182, total 584 plus 15 vagrants.

Vagrants were travelling people who would receive a meal and a night's lodgings for doing a certain amount of work. They would have been in the workhouse on the day of the census. School blocks and officers' accommodation were added behind the infirmary in 1883 but were converted to infirmary blocks in 1896 and by 1900 the workhouse had accommodation for 832 paupers.

By 1939 the Beverley Road Institution, as it was by then known, had 922 beds including the hospital and mental wards. Mr. Alex Marshall was the Master and Miss Theodora Ferguson SRN was the Matron and Superintendent Nurse.

The Institution became the Kingston General Hospital in 1948 and in the 1970s the entire front range of buildings were demolished to provide space for the new Day Hospital. The entire hospital was demolished in 2002 and in September 2003 the Endeavour High School opened on the same site.

Sculcoates Union Workhouse 1904
Courtesy of Paul Gibson

Endeavour High School. Present day workhouse site 2007
H & D LHRG

SCULCOATES 1945 AS A CHILD

As a child of six living in Sculcoates in 1945 it certainly was an adventurous place.

If there had been an Air raid we did not have to go to school the next day. We would have spent the night in Clifton Street communal shelter in the school playground with friends and neighbours playing Ludo and Snakes and Ladders. Others doing their party pieces - magic acts and singing. I well recall it was the first time I had seen a packet of cigarettes that squirted water!

At home we slept downstairs in a bed surrounded by railway sleepers, erected by my Dad, (a little claustrophobic at times) in case the house collapsed as it was a very old property.

We could not wait to get out in a morning to collect shrapnel and look for shells and bullets. One day there was a line of bullet marks on the pavement near our front door – it made you realise how close they had been.

The foundry down Cannon Street, where they made cannons for the battle of Trafalgar, had been demolished and it was such an adventure playground for us kids with mountains of cog wheels and engines to explore and treasure to swap.

A large garage on Beverley Road was flattened – but a child could get into the cellar if he knew about it and was sworn to secrecy, it was an "Aladdin's Cave" of headlights, pistons and wheels. A stock of nuts and bolts were found and a technique developed that two screwed together trapping four match heads and thrown, would frighten the life out of any little widow passing.

There was a Balloon Squadron on land down Norfolk Street – always good for entertainment watching them being inflated as four men tried to control it against the wind from knocking nearby chimney pots down.

One day a German bomber crashed in Spencer Street and we all climbed into the 'Cockpit' having the time of our life but nobody ever stopped us, 'health and safety' had still to be evolved.

The National History Museum was bombed down Albion Street and the next day we were all there rummaging through the damage – bashing each other with rare tropical birds from the damaged display cabinets – again nobody stopped us, a definite case of vandalism. I think looking for anybody in the debris was more a priority.

There was no street lighting, but I don't remember any street crime. But I do remember it was the time I saw my first banana, and my mother would insist she made it into one of her 'doorstep' sandwiches for more nutrition!

I was evacuated to live with an aunt but it only lasted three days because I cried all the time and they sent me home. I'm glad they did, for life was full of adventure and we were never bored.

A former Sculcoates resident.

BIBLIOGRAPHY

Allison, K.J. (Ed) *Victoria County History of Yorkshire, East Riding, Volume One*

Oxford (1961)

Barnard, H.C. *A History of English Education from 1760*

London (1961)

Barnard, Robert *A History of Further Education in Hull*

Hull (1966)

Barnard, Robert *Rough Notes on Wincolmlee Pubs*

Hull (1998)

Cook. J.N.O. *History of God's House in Hull*

Hull (1882)

Credland, Arthur G *The Hull Whaling Trade – an Artic Enterprise*

Cherry Burton (1995)

Curry, Robert *The Last Complete Performance. In memory of Hull's cinemas* Hull (1992)

Egerton, S *Housing on Humberside*

Hull (1989)

Foster, Bernard *Living and Dying. A Picture of Hull in the Nineteenth Century.* Hull (1984)

Geraghty, T *A North-East Coast Town. Ordeal and Triumph* Hull (1955)

Gibson, Paul & *Lost Pubs of Hull* Hull (1999)
Wilkinson, Graham

Gillett, E. &	*A History of Hull*	*Hull (1989)*
MacMahon, K.A.		
Gould, Christine &	*Sculcoates Ancient and Modern*	
Knapp, Donald		*Hull (1991)*
Hadley, G.	*New and Complete History of the*	
	Town and County of	
	Kingston-upon-Hull	*Hull (1778)*
Ketchell,	*Hull Board Schools*	*Hull (2004)*
Christopher		
Lubbock, Basil	*The Artic Whalers*	*Glasgow(2004)*
Markham, John	*Streets of Hull*	*Beverley (1987)*
	The Book of Hull. The Evolution of	
	a Great Northern City	*Buckingham(1989)*
Morfitt, Paul &	*Hull Tramways*	*Midhurst (2005)*
Wells, Michael		
Neave, D	*Lost Churches and Chapels of Hull*	
		Hull (1991)
Needler, Raymond	*Needler's of Hull*	*Cherry Burton (1993)*
Pevsner, Nikolaus	*The Buildings of England, Yorkshire:York*	
& Neave, David	*and The East Riding*	*London (1995)*
Pugh, B	*The Hydraulic Age, Power Supplies*	
	before Electricity	*London (1980)*
Richardson, John	*The Local Historian's Encyclopedia*	
		New Barnet (1993)

| Rowley, Jennifer C. | *The Hull Whale Fishery* Lockington (1982) |

Sheahan, J.J. *History of the Town and Port of Kingston-upon-Hull* Hull (1864)

Tickell, J *History of the Town and County of Kingston-upon-Hull* Hull (1796)

Watson, Roger *Edwin Chadwick, Poor Law and Public Health* London (1969)

Woolley, William *A Collection of Statutes Relating to the Town of Kingston-upon-Hull...to the End of the Reign of George IV* London (1830)

Anglo-Saxon and Viking Humberside (Humberside County Council)

Bulmer's Directory of East Yorkshire for 1892

The City of Hull Official Handbook for 1908

The transactions of the Georgian Society for East Yorkshire, 1955-56

Kelly's Directory of Hull for 1939

Various papers from the Christopher Ketchell Collection with particular reference to the Property portfolio for Sculcoates Power Station and the electric power chronology of 1992

Power from Piped Water: a Century of Victorian Genius. The New Statesman (July 1977)

Ordnance Survey maps

ACKNOWLEDGEMENTS

Albert Rollinson, Arthur Tonkinson, Beryl Taylor, Christopher Ketchell, Cllr Mark Collinson, Cllr Michael Ross, Daniel Hands, David Smith and the staff of the Hull Local Studies Library, David Wilson, Dee Williamson, Elaine Bates, Fran McStay, Gareth Watkins, Hillary Sigg and Jean Whittaker for the information regarding schools, Holmes Hall Tanners, Hull & District Local History Research Group, Hull Daily Mail, Hull Times, Jackie Wright

Jacqui Cole, Kelly Woodall, Kerrie White, Lucy Jackson Margaret Anderson, Winifred Collinson, Colleen Foster, Jean Harrison, Eve Rands, Nicky Gelder, Pam Green, Pat Sullivan Paul Gibson, Rev. John Leeman, Rev. L.S. Deas, Master of Hull Charterhouse, R.W.Leake, Rob Robinson, The Beverley Road Community Wardens, Tracey Toner, The Dorchester Hotel, Hull, The Newland Ward Local Police, The staff of the Brynmor Jones Library, University of Hull, The staff of the Hull City Archives, Tony Saxby, Yorkshire Post.

1928 Ordnance Survey

105